MARTYR

Kathleen Woolrich

Kathleen Woolrich Books
2018

First Printing:

EAN: 9780578419015
ISBN: 0-578-41901-7
ISBN-13: 978-0-578-41901-5

Kathleen Woolrich Books
Orlando, FL, USA

Dedication

To the people of Algeria and Morocco thank you.
To my mother and brother and children. I love you. This is my
heart. Martyr.

Thank you. Without your support and patience, I would have
never achieved my dream.

.

Contents

Acknowledgements

I would like to thank all my Algerians and Moroccan friends without whose help this book would never have been completed.

Martyr

I shall hang on the cross you built for me
I shall wash the wounds you beat into my skin
I shall dream the nightmares you built for me
I shall be the martyr
Of all your fears and dreams
I shall be the martyr to hang on the cross you built for me
I shall be the biggest whore
The worst woman
The object of all your anger
I shall be the martyr
I shall scream in pain, till everything that breaks me disappears
I shall be the child in the corner, the wife in the closet, the scapegoat
I shall be the martyr
I was at the end of your fist
I was the girl who carried her child and placed him in the grave
I will be the one you blame. I will be the one you shame
But I will come back for you
I will haunt your every dream
I will sail through your dreams above your bed
For every time you beat me , I will scream your name
In your sleep, in your dreams, when you work, when you walk
I will be the one you did not kill
I will be your martyr

Avenged

You turned the page
I burned the book
I will be avenged
You let down your guard
I picked up my sword
I say revenge revenge
You turned the page
I burned the book.
I will baby be avenged
You dropped the ball
I picked up a bat
Its time baby for revenge
You left the room
I torched the house
I wont let you leave me for dead
You moved on
I moved out
Now all i hear in my head
Is you turned the page
I burned the book.
You turned the page
I burned the book

The Hierarchy of Sound

its the hierarchy of sound
its the basis
for a river of torment that flows through me
its a rage against the minutes its a feeling
Its a closure of the grave its tranquilty

Its the hierarchy of sound
its the soldiers
its the liberation of souls
its desperation
in the souls of the followers its the freedom
to erase their shattered hearts its liberation

Come find the sound come find the end
You ll kill your very soul with the pain you feel inside
you will rise on the melodies and impale yourself as you follow the
hierarchy of sound

Drowning

Slipping underwater
Baby I am drowning
Grab my hands.. Im holding them for you to grab
Needing you to save me
The black water envelopes me
I can t breathe and I can t speak
come find me in the river

theres a church beside the water
I walked too far and walked into it
Rocks my the pockets of my coat to way me down
As I walk in the currents are swirling and they will carry me away

I am slipping underwater
I am drowning in my grief
I cannot fine my way back to shore
save me baby save me
I need you to break the waters
with your hands your touch your love
I am drowning in the river and I cannot reach the shore

I Have a Skeleton Heart

Bones wrapped around my heart
I have a skeleton heart
Hard where it should be soft
And blood cant move any more
I used to let tears leave my eyes
Let my heart run free
But now its scarred and bony
No open soft place. No open door
baby i got a skeleton heart
its halloween every time I close my eyes
I miss you so . Im haunted so
I cant have you but I cant let go
Because Im holding on with my skeleton heart

My skeleton heart is in your hands.
Broken tormented and lost
Im not sure what ill do to survive you
I paid too much . spoke too much played too much with this skeleton
heart

Greencard

Maybe a little bit too broken
Easy to excuse away
While you craft your devious plan
She never mattered anyway
Divorced or with kids.. just broken enough to be used

Greencard

So as you craft your devious plan
You can tell everyone you tried your best
And tell them all she drank or cheated
When she did nothing of the sort
as you chased your goal

Greencard

What an ugly mess you made
Of her kids and her life
What a sorted tale you told
Full of lies and fakery
All for papers
And permission

To sleep under a bridge

Greencard

The Ruined

I shall be the ruined
Tossed and turned
and woken from a deep sleep
I shall not be redeemed
or loved or saved
I am in danger
And I shall be the ruined
I am so far from home
Unsafe and delusioned

I shall not be redeemed or saved
I am carrying all your sins .. And I shall be the ruined

I shall be the cross you bear.. the name you speak
the tears you shed.
I shall be the last one there... the life you waste
the body you spare..

I shall be the last one left and I shall be the ruined

You discount me..left me for dead
And I shall be the ruined

Outlaw

What do outlaws look like?

Maybe they look like me
Soul raised from the grave
Sleeping souls in the western skies
Ill own those words
Ill sit like Johnny Cash in a cafe in Franklin North Car0lina

I will hold my pencil like Kerouac or watch the tides come in like
Steinbeck

I cannot look out of a prison window.. but I can be an outlaw
Break these chains across my heart and free my outlaw soul

I am an outlaw. I live and die by proxy
Soul raised from the grave
The colors I paint on myself are technicolor

I am a colorless form... I can be black or white or grey and ugly or
beautiful

I am an outlaw

Talking to the Dead

as she rounds the cemetary
round the curves of the gravel road
she talks to her son and daddy
to relieve her heavy load
the pain she carries deep inside
images inside her head
Shes not talking to herself
Shes talking to the dead

Talking to the dead
Oh talking to the dead
Kathleen writes out her memories
And unleashes them insead

Talking to the dead
sweet kathleen Talks to the dead
her heart is clearly broken
And its rough seas up ahead

Theres a cast of shadow on the gates
where she stops to stare
at the pebbles on the driveway
and the steel posts eery glare
This town is only sundown
when her heart begins to break
theres just too many empty evenings
and no chances left to take

Talking to the the dead
Sweet kathleen talks to the dead
her heart is clearly broken

And its rough sees up ahead

Mehdi

Holding onto your grave
its me alone now
you and me
greenwood is just an address and they locked the gates
and I will not escape
a handfull of pills and a quiet car
time wont let me be
I died 10 years ago when you left me
Mehdi mehdi
Holding on to those dreams
in a bed I lie whats left of me
10 years ago we said goodbye
warm water envelopes me
and undeserving undeserving I lost you
Now I am just a slave for the sound that breaks my ears
As tears stream down my face
Blackest metal twisted breaking sounds of guitars fill my brain
As it shakes inside my head
nothing left but me and them
Black metal and death metal
I miss you Mehdi .. I am still in the cemetery even though I am walk-
ing outside the gates
I am my the witness of my own murder
Now just trapped inside black metal and I cannot escape
Mehdi

my my my

if you wanna be bad come be it with me
if you wanna get in trouble come sit by me
we will raise some hell together
Lets get in trouble
Cause you know I dont care
I have metal in my blood
My head was banging being bad since I was 8
with kiss alive 2
I m never scared
What are you waiting for
What the hell do you think you were created for
Motorhead said
What the hell are you waiting for
Lets roll and do this shit
Lets be born to raise hell

Golden But Cannot Say My Name

I am a little too broken
A little too finished
A little too scary even they say the aren't scared of the dark
You ll scream my name in the darkness
I ll save you from the depths of hell
Metal to the core
But you cannot love me in public, because I am just too much of an outlaw
I can take it
I can be the back door girl
The one who saved your soul in private
And knows your crimes and dreams
So I am a little too broken
You never were the bad ass you thought you were
I am the bad ass

I am the one who made mistakes and has to live with them, walk through humiliation and keep on going
So reduce me to what was left to value
My curves, my lips, my face, my surface
Because I am the bad ass
I am the only who ll scream against my fears and scream against what breaks me
And love without boundaries and love without fear
Holy diver and The game and ever small clue to who I was and what I needed

Ill save your soul in private
But in public I am just a little too broken for your taste
Golden but you cannot say my name

Malevolant

Take me to the church of your evil
Your eyes are black as night and you becon me
To walk across the bridge, over your moat and into your arms
Ma LE VOLENT
All you want is a body count
All you need is more bodies spent
In the worship of your evil face
You haunt each space of my heart

Ma levvvvvvvvvvvvvvvvvvvvvv o lent
Walking death, thats all you are
Eating my heart and chewing me and spitting me out
Wait for daylight and finish your deeds
As she loves you, I fulfill your needs
Ma Levvvvvvvvvvvvvvvvvvvv o lent

Lose my number, lose my name
Leave me out of your evil game
Take away what pain you deal
I already know you arent real
All you are is Malevolent

Malfeasance is the gift you give
Trickery and coldness is how you live
You break hearts like toys but I know you
And theres nothing else but evil in your eyes to give
Malfeasant

You made me into a witch to deal with your spells
So open up your eyes baby I am sending you straight to hell

Because all you are is MALEVVVVVVVVVVVVVVVVVOLENT

Never Your Kind of Girl

I am the one who can reach inside of you
Know your dirty secrets and crimes
But you know that even with all that
I was never your kind of girl
I am the one you'd shame and lecture
Tell me how I made mistakes and which door I should have left
closed
Counted all my mistakes and read them back to me
I was never your kind of girl
Now you want to point out the obvious
Make list after list in your head of why I am like I am
I am the wreckage of two or three bad turns
A fiery inferno of a misspent life
An example of everything a woman should not do
And I was never your kind of girl
How about this?
You were never that kind of man
Stick your list up your ass and sit back down
I never needed another list or boss
I needed a man who could set me free
Let me slide beneath the sheets and be vulnerable
So seriously fuck you and your rules, your conventions and your lec-
tures
I don't need a list of things I will never be
I won't buy into your list of impossible hurdles
I'll keep my bag of clothes with my broken heart
I'll put whatever I have left back into the bag
My heart my soul my needs and my dreams
Because I was never your kind of girl

Maestro

Take away my pain
I need to hear Dahamane
Break my eyes and make them cry as you hold the candle
You are the only one who can reach me ya Djamel
As you peel years from my face with your music
and Take me the place I need to go
As I sit in a chair in Algiers
As the drums play
I drift away to 1968 and theres a man there that plays for me
The zina girl with the lost look in her eyes
Ya Djamel break my heart with your guitar
the maestro

What's this mess?
Wesh nu hidaya?
This mess we are in?
It is sure not love. I am not sure it is even like.
It might be hate. It might be passion.
It might not be anything
Wesh nu hidaya?
Is it adoration?
Are we bored?
I think we are both wasting our time
Boiling our lives like over cooked vegetables
Let s call it a day
 A nap would be better
Than love wrapped in confusion and maybe weird friendship
Wesh nu hidaya? Wesh?

Unreachable

Sometimes I open up and share my heart
I pour my truth out in front of me
And when its not taken care of
I just feel shattered
I am unreachable
Like a ship upon the water
I cannot reach or touch the sails
And nothing I write seems beautiful
Khallouni galbi
Khallouni
Let me be
Its too late.. I am unreachable

Algeria Take Whats Left

I do not have my health anymore
Time is short and I've run out of goodbyes
Please take whats left
Take my tears and my time
and make my life a bridge for your children
Take my last years and time here and help me a fountain for your children
Take my blood and take my hands.. take my clothes and take my fears
Take whats left of me Algeria.. pick clean my bones I owe my life to you
Hold my tears and hold my arms
I love you so Algerie
Devoted like Amirouche and held to you like Harrachi

I hold you close like a statue watching the ocean
Forever vigilant.. Kahina on the rocks
I owe you so
You are my destiny and my good byes and hello
So when I see you again Ill hold the soil beneath me and say
I came back. I came back. I came back to Algerie
And stayed forever devoted .. through loss and death
Through good byes and sadness
I returned to you. .. Bledi. I returned to you
Your adopted daughter
I will be Kahina on the mountain
I will be Djamila in the Casbah
I'll be the watcher in the night
Carrying your children to safety all over the world
You remain my beloved
Algeria

Love You Without A Happy Ending

It cant and wont happen
the stars did not align
It wont work and cant work
But I can watch the stars with you
And we can figure out what never was and can never be and smile
And I can love you with no happy ending
No final words no final good thing for me
Just the memory that I loved you and you loved me
And love you without a happy ending
All the goodbyes were said the minute I met you
and the clock started ticking
But it was worth every moment I never could hold onto
I loved you with no guarantees
I loved you with no happy ending

I Bleed the Words

I begin to type or write
and words flow out of me like victims
some willing

Saying Khallouni khallouni
they speak in dardja or arabic
and they tell me I long for you Kathleen
set me free in sentences and in words and like Algerians walking
smoking
looking for a coffee

My poems wrap around buildings
smashing coffee cups on tables or folded like a newspaper
always precise or careless
whatever mercurial mood

My words are Algerian. My words are no longer English
They say Galbi. They say Rabbak

They say a thousand angry but possesive words

I am a poet possssed
in El biar
I am lost somewhere in Audin
Possessed by Algerian djinns
or lost cofffee seekers

I bleed upon tables or the ground
I am stuck in kharouba
or maybe just against a wall in the casbah

Possessed

Thimouchouha

I want to tell a story
of when I loved you and you loved me
and all we had was the air in the room
and the days that left us... they have all grown cold

I want to tell a story
Of Jugurtha
And Massinissa and Kahina
and a million days gone by
and I could walk down from the mountain and burn all the trees
And imagine I am a queen and the hills were on fire

thimouchouha

and a million words between us
I could love you but I will not
I could remember but I cannot
I will just burn all the hills and cast myself off a cliff

And tell myself thimouchouha
Till I sleep
and grieve and tumble down the hills

thimouchouha

Avghigh akhdinigh thamacahout.
Ghaf Assan asmi nemyahmal
Ghafasmi ournass3i ala thakhamth ifarghan ,
Ouk thoussan ighyajane rouhan.
Yeqimd oukham dhassamadh,
Avghigh akhdahkough
Thamachahout anjugurtha
Thamachahout an massinissa
Thamachahout an kahina.
Thamachahout na boussane ighyajane rouhen,

......
Avghir awandahkugh themushuha

1000 Tears

I stored you up inside of me like a bank
10 for my son who died
10 for the time I came home to an empty home, sofars overturned
10 for a slap or a punch or some spit
and 10 for the time another woman laid in my bed
I will try to replace those tears with sunshine and flowers
But right now open the gates
I will let them flow
So come with me tears and flow like wine
I will cry and cry until the tears cannot hurt me
I will cry from Algiers to Tlemcen
To Chaabi and rai and all music in between
I will cry from Casablanca to Tanger and all stops in between
Till those 1000 tears run dry
1000 tears

The End of the Story

Your dinner is cold
and so is my heart
this warm embracing flesh that girds my breasts
has become ice cold
You are now just a memory even in front of me
I cooked and cooked and put love into each
cake and piece of meat I cooked
And I tried over and over again
But you failed me

So here is where we are
Your dinner is cold and so am I
As I stand in the kitchen looking at a plate of food that turned to ice
As you were with everyone else but me

So your food is cold
and now so am I
As I turn out the light, and cover the food
I do not want to talk about it
I do not forgive you
The clock started ticking
towards the end of you and me

Your dinner is cold
And so am I

Momentum

For Bel Ange

Set me free as we dance upon the water
The cold does not own us and we shall run into the shore
the water wrapping around our ankles
Summer is upon us and everything we used to dream of
Has become the sugar of our lives
Momentum
Wind and rain and the cold does not not hurt us much
For we are a house
And we move together in unity
In love and in momentum
I love you and you love me
Nothing is dark with you by my side

Momentum

Sweet Prince

Tomorrow was not promised
And as the car came with you
I stood there and they opened the door

My head full of all the stories about you
How kind you were and who you were to everyone

Goodbye sweet prince
Take care along the miles
Across the skies as you travel back to them
To the country that I love but cannot stay besides

You are a child of the bled
My darling beloved country
Take care across the skies beloved son
I stood as they took you to wait to leave and I was alone and I told
you
It will be ok
You will return to the lions of Oran
and the strong brave Algerians I adore

I was your lion of Orlando
Thank you for blessing my life with your goodbye

We love you

Good bye from America our sweet prince

Haunted

Sunday, October 25, 2015

Every light in the house is on
the doors all unlocked but still I freeze
because the dreams come back again to stay

and I will not make it out of this haunted house

I am haunted you see and I cannot let go
of each time I felt I was safe and was proven wrong

Each time I thought life was going to mine and things would be ok
The winds just blow and blow me back through the door of this
haunted haunted house

So the ghosts became my friends and the darkness my light
And black my rainbow and solitude the norm
And I am going to stay here.. love me or not

Wait or not.. Ill still stay in here.. this haunted house.. this haunted
house

This haunted house is me... the curtains will stay drawn.. even in the
lightest warmest day
I'm just a haunted heart...I'm just a haunted frame of wood
A ladder.. a broken window for eyes...

And you will maybe come inside and join me

but sometimes when my face glosses over and I look like I'm some-
where else

I'm just inside myself

inside the haunted house
inside my haunted heart

closing my haunted eyes

I am a haunted house

Clochard

I dont love you anymore
Its so hard how love leaves
It leave with a few words
then bad behavior
and all we are left with are the clowns we become
Clochard.. we are ... a clochard for all seasons
we enter the winter of love
that started with summer and ended up with brokeness
Some replace lost love with another
Id rather dig a well and toss myself into it
Walech del ghadar walech
I dont love you anymore
I dont dislike you I just dont care
And I want to be alone
Some pine for lost people, Id rather not.
Id rather burn all your pictures and bury the ashes
I dont need your help, your friendship or your memories
Im not the type to be unkind but I cant see a single thing about you
anymore that ties you to me
You are not kind or generous
You make me sad
Id rather be alone than with a liar
Or be made to cry for no reason at all
I just dont love you any more
One day you ll know what I was but I wont care
I already don t anyway
there are lines we don t cross and you crossed all I had left
All I am is suffering now and wishing you were gone
You are here but I
Im not
I dont love you anymore

I dont miss you anymore
I dont miss your smell or your touch

I dread the sight of you.
I dont wait for kindness. I just wait for loss.
You used to be the light in my sky.
Now you are just breaking me down into whatever left you can take
Or using me till you can accomplish your goals and short term
salvation
All you are is a ghost
I cant see you anymore

I dont love you anymore

What The Wind Blew Away

Sunday, September 17, 2017

those of us who have held loved ones
as they passed
or have been beaten or bloodied
we were never blew away
we watched the sky come down and take our things
take our security
the waters rise up to our ankles and to our waists
Or our houses rip apart
and we knew as the trees fell and the winds raged

that were never lost

As I gathered my photo graphs and my things and my family
and waited to ride out the storms

that I was going to be the one who knew
that I had all I needed close to me
And I would never be one of the things
the wind blew away
Like
Commen

I Ran Out of Words

I ran out of words to say to you
Because there is no point in continuing the conversation
It will not turn into I love you
It can never be anything
And while the chemistry between us makes the air heavy
There is no sense in continuing
I ran out of all the words to say to you
I have haunted eyes and a haunted heart
I do not have the time to figure out how to maneuver around you
I ran out of words to tell you
I ran out of words

To The Lovers

I've never been on to feel anything but glory
Glory in the sky and light all around
When I see two people fighting the evil of this world and all the no
words in this world
to love
Love fiercefully and with your blood

Love without abandon
And leap from the cliff into the water
If you begin to drown, it might crush you
But if you float, or even falter, love will be there

You must be brave in the face of the people who say
Love does not exist!
It does
As surely as many will not believe
It will find you in the darkness
It will buoy you in the storm
It will hold in you in the coldness of life
Dear lovers don t despair
Find each other and say I love you
Don t let go of hope and plunge into sadness
And if you are a person that love evaded
Walk towards the light and realize it will come for you again
Don t despair
You can drink every drink and smell every flower in the garden of
love
Just take the seeds in your hand and till the soil
And be kind and good and lovable
And know , just know that love and goodness will always prevail
And roses come back from the cold and winter

Truth Was All We Had

Once upon a time
Truth was all we had
It was all we owned or held or spoke and ate and drank
But life got complex and the lines were blurred
And now all we swallow are half truths and nonsense

So mix me up an elixir so that I can see
What has evaded me for years and I chased cognition
Truth as all we had darling and now all we have is nonsense
I cannot bear to speak to you
If all you do is lie
Conjecture . manipulate.. and play a few games
No truth is left so I must go
Truth was all we had.. but there is none to had now

Truth was all we had

The In Between Life

February 8, 2016

There were apologies I never got
But I had to keep on going, in the in between life
There were people I had to bury and had to continue on and could not wait
For a miracle
In the in between life, in the in between life
Those days sandwiched in between dreams and loss
And life and death
lives the days of the in-between life
Those days where you realise that you just have to keep on going
To live between mounds of laundry and every day chores
To live for the days that you will see the things you dream of
And your life will be restored to times without loss
And your days will be long and sunny again
And those days come, they do, sometimes sparsley, sometimes almost rare indeed
But you learn to love the days of the in between life
You learn to adore the times tucked between the days of glory and laced with sugar
You learn to remember the happier days and hold on to the grittiness of the in between life
To which we all belong in one way or the other
To days in which the normal lies, the in between days
Days of cleaning and cooking and toiling and working
The in-between days in which real life lies
The In Between life days
The in between life

A Skeleton You Built

A skeleton you built

You took my fleshed out love
And you burned me
As if nights with you could keep my heart fed
You boiled by bones with your words
And broke my feelings with your lack of caress

A skeleton you built.. a skeleton you built
nights at Audin

I remember I remember
Before the hammer of life came down

First came the heat of a forgotten summer
And the winds of Algiers that pushed you to me
No longer blue
A skeleton you built oumri
A skeleton
My bones lay on Place Audin

With a thousand stars to witness
A skeleton you built beloved.. a skeleton you built

Where The Cold Comes In

There's a door, close it tight
That is where the cold comes in
It seeps under the door, so slam it shut
Nail it all around the edges
For that is how the cold comes in
It makes me weep, it makes me shake, keep the cold off my skin
Cover me in cloth and keep me warm
Look at that door!
That is where the cold comes in
Keep the drafts away from my fragile heart
And keep me warm
Keep me warm
I've been a fool for love and for the cold
And now its time to stay warm and safe
That door is where the cold comes in

All That Matters Now

Wednesday, April 27, 2016

All that matters now..

Is that life you decided to live today

You can hang on to to the epitaph they decided to write

but I choose rejoice
I choose life with love layered on top
I choose redemption with fire and strength blended in
All that matters now is the fact you stand back up

When you lay prostate forward

That push towards ascension

All that matters now is you breath
And you took a shallow breath
Stand.... darling stand...walk two steps

Its all that matters now..

Its all that matters now

Letter to the Resistance

Wednesday, January 25, 2017

Broken and tired
Dreams burning and fear
But there is no testimony without a test
Trials are where mere mortals become kings
It's easy to read about resistance
It's harder to live through it
So pick yourself up and wash your face
It's a battle you will have to fight and days you will have to endure
The moral compass of the country is not a birthright it's a choice
And you might be the only one out of 50 who says. No Not I. I will
not be part of this

So a letter to the resistance
You are in the middle of moving history.
Things will be turbulent they will be scary
But as MLK said the arch is very long but justice will arrive

Breathe deeply, resist and resist again
And know God will be with you
Against fascism, tyranny and certain evil

Resist, go forth resist

Boumerdes

twists and turns
then Thenia.. then Zemmouri

and I crowned you Bourmedes
I heard Russian in the winds
And then I saw your face how you shown white and blue and yellow
As small boats tossed in the harbor
I stopped and ate potatoes and chicken with cheese
And drank cold gazzouz as the sun shone
I stopped to greet the fishing boats and took pictures with my eyes
Click click click

It Was Never About That

When I fell in love with North Africa
It was never about a guy.. or tangible things

It was never about that
It was about the blues and the yellows
It was about the tea
It was about how beautiful I felt when I stood in the window on the
8th floor
of the apartment in Ghermoul
It was about the fish I ate in Tanger
and how the sky looked when i was outside in Ain Diab
It was about the bus station at Kharouba
And how it felt to be surrounded by people from 20 different cities
It was never about a person
It was never about an individual
The love was about the liberation I felt
The songs I heard
The books I read
Choukri, Yacine, Djaout
The languages
The love ... the emotional salvation
Dahmane El Harrachi

The flowers of Telemely
The streets of Setif
The sky in Tanger

the way the water looked at Las Oudayas
but it was never about a person
It was about the reds at Marrakech
and the tagine at Ourika
and the dark nights in Casablanca
the hospital in Setif

the eyes of my friends
But it was never about what people thought or told me
Every reason is inside of me

The answers to why and how
It was never about that

Love Wins

How can you walk against insurmountable odds and try again?
Some days fear gets the best of me
And erases the better parts of me
But I am here to say love always wins
It wins because even though I have felt pain
And loss and sometimes abandonment
I am here to say love always wins
I rejoice in its victory
And in each memory of everything that went right
In each haunted moment, love always wins
It wins against the brokenness
It wins against the risk of loss
It rises from the pavement and in each tear that falls
Love wins again and again. Love wins against the cold hard ground
It wins against betrayal.. It wins against fear ...love wins

People ask me. How can you love when you might lose everything in
the end?
How can you walk against insuromountable odds and try again?
I try because the risk of not loving is greater than a broken heart
I love because not loving is a greater tragedy than losing everything I
might have to gain
I dance because standing still hurts more than falling
Loving is worth anything I have to lose by trying

So in the end love wins
It wins my darling
Take my arms and take my eyes
Take my soul and take my words
Take each time I cry and taste each tear

For they belong to you

Because I tried and loved and even if I lose, I lived
Love has to win .. it has to win
Because without love , life is an empty tomb
Love wins
Love wins inside each memory
Love wins inside each hello and goodbye

And although other lovers might be more worthy
This is my gift to you

My words will become an anthem and no matter where the chips may
fall
I told you that I loved you
I loved you without abandon
I risked everything to love you
To hold you.. to adore you
And name each moment without abandon
And tell you that love simply wins
It wins even when we are losing
It wins when even we are not loved back
It wins against the wind.. it wins against the storms
It wins when life destroys it
It wins beloved .. it wins
It wins with each tear I cry
It wins with every day I remember all the reasons I loved you
It wins over and over and over again

love
simply
wins
Love wins

Withered Yet Blooming

Let me show you the dying rose
With beige and pink and she is leafy green
But her roots are withering, dying, not embracing water
She's withered yet blooming
Here and there and everywhere
The fight inside is the life's blood
Her bloom the result of life's steps
Let me show you the dying rose
Petals about to fall but smiles serenely
At a grey sky, searching for blue points
She's anchored but falling
Tethered yet drifting
Unsure if beauty was ever in her trove
Let me show you the rose

Do Not Come Look For Me

If you could not stand beside me
And you let the tigers bite
Do not come look for me
I already left and am far away
When the nights are cold and you are alone

And you chose every single person but me

I am not here anymore.. You ll see the shape of my face
Maybe see a shadow me
But if I was not worth protecting or saving,, do not come look for me
Do not mourn my illness
Do not feign affection
Just let me go
But remember when the nights are cold and you are alone
I am no longer here to find or talk to
Do not look for me

Do not look for me

We Closed The Door... Or Did We

I said goodbye and packed my things

I said it's over and left the room
But did we close the door?
Did we say all that we needed to?
Well it's too late for regret.. Because I can't carry your pain

Take it back to Algeria and own your own life
Ill hold on to the ghorba and my simple mind and life
We closed that door.. now lose my number
Forget my name and forget each day
Wipe it out of your mind because I am no longer there
To talk to, to speak about.. I am dead to you....so move along

We closed that door or did we...

Moujahid

So you walk when you cant
You stand when you feel like falling
You keep your lips tightly closed when you want to break
You are channeling their power and their strength

Kathleen be like Djamila Like Ali and stand strong
Resist and stand up and hold the walls of the burning building
Hold whatever pride you have left and do it all for the niff.. for the
purpose of courage
And be like a moujahid
Be a lion in the darkness
Be a leader in the battle
Reach behind you like the ones who walked into the fire
Run the casbah in your mind and be forever brave
You are Algerian by spirit if not by birthright in pain and in trauma,
you reach for their strength
They will sustain you.. their memories and the fight in their faces
Moujahid
Moujahid
Moujahid

Halcyon Days

Wednesday, December 7, 2016

we never knew
we were dancing in starlight
drinking freedom
and holding on to hope

they were the halcyon days
before the winter came
sun filled summers before they pulled the curtain down on us
they were the days of mercy and hope
we never knew were running against time
that love and joy were flags we could fly
against the winter that was coming

And I held your hands and we stood and shouted against injustice
Now they are just the days that run behind us
Now oppression and the oppressors are looming in the distance
winters written our name down and we might not see the spring again
halcyon days and a million days gone by
the sadness steeps like a tea
our resolve binds out hands and thought
to endure the winter and return
to other days and other brighter thoughts
Halcyon days

The Best I Ever Had

He called... with tears in his eyes and a sound in his voice

You were the best I ever had. I miss you so. Im sorry I left
My heart ache doesnt have a home

I thought a minute and said... Go back to Algeria...Theres nothing left
to talk about. You are never coming back to me. Like a sea shore
whos sand has shifted. it was a moment in time I loved you

But you are gone.. You have to stay gone. Go to Setif . Go to
Constantine. Forget you ever knew me

But youll never be back in my life

I am a ghost.. Im a dream.. I m your hope but Im not yours anymore
Ill remember you and try as hard as I cant to pretend I never knew you

Cry in your grave.. and know Ill never make a home with you

Nothing to see here. No one left to call on.. The day you drove away...
I buried my heart and knew Id never return
So look at your memories in your mind. Search the world Im gone.

And She Drove Away

When she sat still and tried to follow
She became a mere copy of herself
But her power came when she drove away
When she drove away, they saw her
When she stayed close, they ignored her
So here's my lesson to the women that behaved
Drive away.. drive far .. go wherever your heart desires.. no one will love you more if you sit
Drive far away.. fill up the gas tank and disappear
Life will not wait for good behavior and you will wake up alone and a lesser person
So drive away and play the music very loud
And write whatever you want because life will not wait for you
Buy the perfume you want and drink what you like
Smell the sea and smell the ocean and let the sand land under your feel

No one will notice when you decide not to move
Live your life like an anthem and drive wherever you want

All I wanted Was A Happy Ending

Thursday, November 12, 2015

Everything right.. was the way she played the game
Do right be kind and look for the light because if you do right right
comes back to you
But sweet queen, it does not work like that
If you are kind, you are stupid
If you are good, you must be unworthy
And if you cry, your tears are a bother not a sign that you are true or
commited
All I wanted was a happy ending
A place of my own and time in the sun
But it did not work out that way
I became a clown in the circus
Or on the beach wearing my clothes, heavy from salt and sand
A queen Ill never be.. Yet I carried the burdens of queens
Expected to shelter and be a stand up kind of girl
But undeserving of a jacket when I was cold or safety when I was
scared
So Ill play the cards that fate has dealt me
A cruise to nowhere.. nothing to eat.. nothing left on the table for me
Because I was too naive to realise
That the more I want a happy ending , the less deserving of it I
became
So close the curtains and close the blinds
I need sleeps silent carriage
To take me somewhere else so I can heal
Away from sound and fright and everything awful
A deep dark blanket to help me forget
that all I ever wanted
was a happy ending

Gates of The Garden

Thursday, June 8, 2017

Who decides when the garden is closed?
I built and I built and dug and dug
I planted and yet the flowers in my garden run wild
I'm now a prisoner even to the flowers
Close the gates , I'm tired
The fountain , turn it off and let it be covered like Jardin D'Essais was
the story of the flowers is at its end
Ill close the gates and stop digging I am tired
The Algerian rose won't wither
There will more to love and enter her doors and they will love her just
like me
The Algerian rose is wild and free
Beloved and sweet smelling.. fierce and strong
Thank you dear rose for the love you have given me
Watching you bloom and move through the vines when heavy rains
hit you
But me I am tired I am locking the gates. I'll write until my hands feel
sore and write till I can feel I love you less

But the gates of the garden will close soon and I will be but a memory
and under the grass I'll rest

Forever in love with my Algeria

The One Who Tried

have you ever been the one who tried
who fought and went down with the ship
there were ones who didnt and somehow they are always safe
the ones who try get swallowed
So heres to being the one who tried
the one who is looked back on and remembered
If I bury the ones who couldnt see that I was the one who loved
the one who dreamed and the one who fought
Then thats just where they have to remain
I am the one who tried
I am the one who wept
I was the last one standing over and over again
Maybe it wasnt good enough
That I fought through illness to make things real
That I fought against good byes and time to do what was right
And got left behind while you chased everything else but me
Ill never know whether I was wrong or right
For being the one who tried

Piece of Me

She's a piece of me
Half Moroccan.. and half of me
And all of herself
Sassy and opinionated.. creative and emotional
Kind and outspoken
She's a miracle and fun
She accompanies me shopping and we go on adventures
She's willing to learn and we read and we try
To learn about Anne Frank's attic and the secrets of Algiers
Moroccan by blood, she loves her people
She loves my people too and asked me to tell her everything I know about FDR
She's a piece of me. She's a piece of them.. And I love her and I love her people
So don't tell me she's entitled when she cries because she tired
And don't run her down to me because she's my baby
She's a piece of me, this smart little girl
Who I treasure and adore

A gift from God to break the loneliness
and the empty spaces
the wind field rooms

My Zahra my flower keeps me company and I adore her
She's a piece of me

ALGIERS, January 2016

Burn It Down

Monday, October 5, 2015

take everything ive written
and burn it in a fire
and take my words and what I thought was prose
and use it as kindling
I thought I had a building
but it was built on sand
I can tell you a thousand reasons why

I know its not my house
its not my house because when I am in in it

the words are just to plaster the walls

some to amuse and some to reflect but I don't want them anymore
so take my prose and all the words I said

and throw them on the fire
if heat was enough to make the words collapse
then break the pens and the letters on the keyboard too
and while youre at it burn my clothes. I dont need them either
burn my books.. my pictures my skins already in flames

because theres nothing left of me

they say they love you and want to save you but in the end you are
left holding an empty hanger

On which maybe a dress woulld hang or maybe more.. maybe my
nose in the middle of my face got too long

so take the words ... and any books I wrote.. and toss them too. and
any papers left that say my name, I dont want them either

i wrote of love and longing.. but it doesnt not have my name.its just nonsense that when placed in fire eviscerates and then theres nothing left

So burn me.. burn my things and stand real tall.. we will light a match until they all are gone..

the words my faith my face and my fate..
to be lied to toyed with and played with like a handful of dice..

so light a match..you go first. and there wil be nothing left of me. Im tired you know.. and broken so

if your fire is hot.. burn one down for me...

take the matches... my books... lets find everything in the house

and make the fire 20 stories high

and on that fire I place each insincere word

each false moment and each burden I carried

Because the scales are tipping my way anyway.. a heavy thump under neath the scales because I gave more.. and in the end I was right I was... despite my fears

It happened so...betrayal..and falsehoods.. Perhaps Ill drink till the fire blows out
who knows darling who knows

But when you torched me.. I silently baked

and if you know fires how they ember on..
if you can do better than 100 percent of truth
and leave me to melt on the floor like hot coals

 but they spread across and shatter the wood on the house that I built with my words

so burn and break and shatter and toss... it matters nothing now If I have no words left
Ill find a way to replace them with other choice sentences... a brittle hot glass it became..

loves bitter burn just turns into glass at the end of the day.. and then its either molten or shatters under the weight of the day
just burn whats left down.. I care no more for words

they are all i have left when people are gone...so damn them too..

and damn myself

let it all burn

The Pirate

In the cradle of Algiers
In a quiet place
Lived the pirate
In a fortress all his own

The pirate with soft steps and a heavy heart he walks
 oh he took the ceiling in his hands and handed it to the moors
he's locked out of the village of his birth
 Oh for the pirate they cry
 But they do not know the pirate will only settle on the seas
dear pirate I know you even though your face turns to black
I know its not black its only shadowed
  So tell me dear Pirate where will you find your solace?
 in the whiteness of other blood or in the scent of your own

Ill leave you to your wreckage dear pirate but know Your secrets are
safe with me
and I will not share the words you speak
So don't worry I won't knock at your door
But some day when the moon is full
Call my name from the street
And we will go a haunting
The pirate

Love is Stronger Than

Saturday, March 26, 2016

Love is stronger than addiction
Love is stronger than the pull to the grave
If the one you love dies, their essence continues
In every leaf that falls, in every song that plays in a darkened room
while a mother cries
Love is stronger than deceit
Love is stronger than rejection
Love is stronger than self abuse
Love is stronger than loss
Love is stronger than goodbye
Love screams I forgive you when wronged
Love paints a normal face every color of the rainbow
In rage, in happiness, in loss

Love is stronger than goodbye , I tell you
It is soaring
Its eternal
Love is stronger than the mistakes we make
Its stronger than misgivings
Its a form of justice all its own
Love exists past all that we suffer
It exists past the coldness of death
Its in every morning when the sun defiantly returns

Love
Is
stronger
than anything that scares you
Believe in it
Love will find you one way or the other, it will comfort you in grief
It will comfort you in loss

Look for her, the angel thats waiting to take a friend or child home again
Or right next to you to tell you do not lose hope
Love is stronger....

Unclaimed

When she died.. I went and claimed her
When things looked murky.... I claimed them
When me and my baby felt scared and lost, North Africans claimed us

There is power when you claim. When you maybe know someone is
not perfect
And you claim.
You say.... THAT IS MINE... you do not say.. well that's kind of a
mess.. Maybe I will look like a mess too... if I provide.. If I say I love
her or him... or it or them.. I claim you....

Everyone wants to claim.. but no ones wants to be strong enough to
claim...unless they have nothing less to love.. they will claim every-
thing.. God.. Danger...sadness loss

So the unclaimed shall be mine.. the unloved.... I will claim them. I
will claim them as my own.. You don't want her or it or them or the
pain. Then do not claim it when its well. Unclaimed....yes we were..
and they and she was .. But then you want it when it benefits you.. Or
them or it... or whatever you would not own.

Claiming is power.. When you declare love, you make it public. You
do not hide it. You claim it
Unclaimed....and left.. and then you watch her or their strength.. And
of course, you want a part of what will help you.. But love is when
you claim and hold and own.. Not leave and come around when per-
haps better days have arrived
So Ill will claim and honor and raise up, all of the good and hide all of
the bad

Because love looks like that. Love looks like acknowledgement. Not shame and hiding.. Not withdrawal

Love looks like a ring. Love looks like a promise. Love looks like a funeral. Love looks like a scrapbook. Love looks like a story ... a poem.. and a wedding. Love looks like a song.. a garden that is carefully mowed. Love does not look like neglect. It looks like a lawn.. It looks like a garden that people took care of. Love does not look like madness and crying and left over ruin

Love looks like care. It looks like claiming. I claim you. You claim me. We claim each other. But if you hide me, no matter what you say..... if you don't honor my life, then you don't love me. You can tell me I love you. You can say I love you. But if you don't tell OTHER people you loved me, you never did.
So I claimed her body, because I loved her. I fought for her . Because she was my best friend and I loved her. I threw parties... We celebrated death and live and everything in between. Because I loved her. I claimed her. Algeria claimed me. I claimed her. Morocco claimed Zahra even though her family did not. You claim when you love. You don't belittle. You don't make people disappear. You don't make them invisible. You claim them

That is love. You can tell me love looks like anything you want it to be. But if love does not involve claiming. If you won't stand by , stand up and stand with, you don't love.. that person.. that thing.... or want that person...
If the claiming is not present, there was and never will be love
Love is claiming.. love is claiming. I proclaim
I proclaim my love, my friendship, my devotion.
You can claim your child, your heritage, your faith or lack their of
But you claim

And love never is
anything
unclaimed

Waiting for Goodbye

You werent all there
And laid your heart open

And let me know I was on borrowed time
Im just waiting for goodbye
Waiting until you have somewhere better to be
Than by my side
You let me know why and how
And I was not ready
But I am now
I am waiting for goodbye
I no longer can relax with you or smile or dream
Or plan or think Ill have another summer
Or winter
Because I am on borrowed time
So when you leave
I ll wipe my mind, my books, my phone my memories that you ever
existed
And let you fade into a song, a night a memory
Since I am waiting for goodbye

You ll figure out 2 months from the day you ll leave
That I might have been all you ever needed or wanted
But it wont matter then.
Because I wont be there any more
I lost my faith
I lost my hope
I lost all interest
When I found out I was waiting for goodbye.

and it was all but over but he stood and said
a little more till they break
and he stood and said I am Amirouche

I am here to make the day into night and the night into day
and some day they will mourn me because I am rajel and strong
some day they will curse me as too brutal and savage
But savage is all I know
Amirouche I understand
Amirouche I understand your steps, your moves and your middle and
your end
and some will never understand the steps we all have to take to have
closure
to sleep in the rocks like Amirouche
to wade in the rivers
and stare into the sun
Amirouche

Did You Learn How to Dance My Love

Did you learn how to love or learn how to dance
From knowing my scent or my voice

Do you have memories of me when you lie awake at night?
You dismissed me as average or invisible
But time told you differently
I was burning with a fire you wont see again
And now you can write your name on every wall
And across the sky with your fingers but I will never return

Did you learn how to dance my love?
The day I said goodbye to you I set both of our souls free
Because I knew the power of goodbye
The smell of the flowers .. the jasmine as I walked beneath it
The Mays the Augusts and Decembers of our lives
Sometimes love is only beautiful looking backwards
And you only learn to dance when you stand alone

Did you learn how to dance my love?

Do you think its strange I wish you well?
Oh dont I wish you nights that are cool and water that is clear
I wish you clouds in the sky. I wish you colors in the ocean that you
can capture in your eyes
I wish you everything well in this world
But I wont be present..
Did you learn how to dance my love?

Sunset Black

Sometimes grief makes the sky three shades of black
Algeria my flag I miss you so
I am miles and miles from you and myself right now
Stuck in a place I can't break out of
Held to the ground when all I want to do is fly
Sunset orange sunset yellow and sunset black
that's all I can see
I can piece together words to say that I'm ok
But I'm painting the sky every color but blue
Black maybe red green or yellow
Angry orange or violent
Or just black and Ill keep painting
Throwing paint at the sky
Till Algeria re appears in my eyes as I lay to sleep
Because she can't come again
Too far gone and too far away... not enough chances to fly again
Sunset black
Sunset blue

I weep and grieve
Take me to her again.. Take me back to Algiers and her bending waist
Her whites her blues her flowers and rocks
Take me back to the water the sky and the stars
Sunset black.. sunset black

Broken Kind of Beautiful

I ve loved way too much too often and with poor results
Ive cried and put my head down because I never thought I could raise
it

But I went to Morocco and Algeria and decided I was a broken kind
of beautiful
My friends from there didn't care that I wasn't successful and perfect
and everything I could or should be

Kathleen you are a broken kind of beautiful they told me. You have
character and you are strong ... they told me

You are a strong woman and a kind woman with a white heart.. they
told me
They told me I was a broken kind of beautiful

That I could hold on and make it and stay calm when I was suffering
When I was sick , two ran through the night in Algiers to get
injections
When I couldn't eat or walk, one picked up my daughter
When I needed a breathing treatment, one slept in my house to watch
my child and go off to school

Ill be your broken kind of beautiful. Ill be that friend that never leaves
Ill be your Cheba Fadela.. your tragic friend..your everything because
you were everything to me

so if you hurt and you cant find your way.. Im here.. My soul is in
North Africa until I can return to her..

Ill be your broken kind of beautiful, my moroccan and algerian
sisters. Ill be that friend that listens and never leaves...
From the mountains of Ourika to the plains of Setif. I left my soul
across the magreb

Im a broken kind of beautiful. a shattered plate thats somehow held together
I love you
I am a broken kind of beautiul

Telemely

Monday, February 8, 2016

The paints were all the colors I feel each day
Blue and Yellow and Red and Green
Not mixed with others into the colors of the fall
And splashed against canvases that hung in a store
Telemely has become
What I dreamed in my sleep
And artists crade and flowers on the streets
For sale
Telemely we are sisters
And If could stand next to you, where the school meets the street

And walk a little bit farther to the museums
I weep with happiness that you again live
And I lived to see you blossom
In the crown of Algiers, we see the split streets
And I look for your oil paint stores
And peer into the artist galleys
And look for flower stands
on the streets of Telemly

I Crown Myself Queen

With head held high
I crown myself queen
Ill take my own robes
And by my own gold
And be powerful and brave
Ill write my way across the pain
And carry words and power within myself
Steady my own gait and be my own hero
Since no one is coming for me

I crown myself queen...
Call Kahina she ll teach me to stand on the mountain
And hold my own when the darkness fills the skies
I am a celt . I can do this...Clan of Tara Irish Ancient blood
Ill choose the warrior path rather than break down
But Ill steady my feet as the earth shakes beneath me
And hold the ground underneath me stepping firmly and carefully

Ill crown myself queen.. since no one else will
Ill claim the power and own it
Ill crown myself queen

Loss Like A River

Thursday, June 2, 2016

Loss like a river
Tears like a torrent
Some things cannot be fixed
No matter how hard we try
They lay broken
Loss like a river
Tears like a torrent

Goodbyes like a package we hold close to our chest
We earn medals for surviving and then become
It's not that we are sad
It's just that the road to the end becomes less paved

Loss like a river
Tears like a torrent

Losses for the brave the true and the solid
It's as if fate chooses the toughest to endure the worst things
And then says move along.. you might have more to carry
So darling loss like a river
tears like a torrent
flowing and flowing till you run dry from the pain
Some will never understand
what they do to you or how it feels
To carry a well spring of tears..
Loss like a river
Tears like a torrent
Goodbyes like a deck of cards.. dropped from your hands one by one
onto the ground
Flipping incessantly.. showing each spade.. each diamond
Dropping in sharp precision one after another
Like a river the tears flow
Perhaps until your face burns
Loss like a river

Tears like a torrent.. until the tears run dry

Heart Like A Wheel

Tuesday, September 13, 2016

Ropes around your heart
Ropes around your ankles
And heart like a wheel

You sold yourself for a ticket out of town
Now you want everything back
Hearts are like wheels but instead of rolling on, they grind forward

So heart like a wheel, the destruction you waged
You feigned love for a ticket anywhere
And she slumped in a corner
a mere body of flesh
with something to take
heart like a wheel

its not about me.. but I saw what you did
to get what you want

Heart like a wheel. you used her so

I saw you

Heart like a wheel

Aïn Diab

Thursday, August 25, 2016

My feet were

as water rushed my legs

in the rocks of Ain Diab

Call and response oh Moroccan call and response

You remember those days? When I might not make it?

I held on to the hope I d pull out of the storm

The winds rose up close to the windows as I drifted in and out
Days grew blurry and left me
And now all I can remember
Is the color of water
The darkness of the night
And how lost I felt
At Ain Diab

Set You Free

I'll own my pain
If it will set you free
I'll tell you who and what hurt me if it will help you be strong enough
to speak out

That that rape you endured does not define you

That the mistakes you made are not a forever thing
That the pain you feel does not separate you from love
That the mistakes you made arent you , they are just things you
endured

That if you hold alcohol close to calm you, there is recovery
If Drugs made you feel better, you can move past them

Whether a person broke you or life broke you
Hold out and hold on

You matter
You are loveable
You are savable
You can save others
You can turn the hands of fate away from someone life has intentions
to batter

That you have talents no matter what your disabilty
that your past is not your today

And if no one told you they loved you, Kathleen does. My voice is
right here

Saying keep going, You can do it. You can stand up
Keep trying . Keep painting your world into a better place

Because your voice is still a voice that can speak
Your life is still a life that is valid and valuable

You are not your past
Ill own my own pain if it will set you free
Now run..throw it all behind you and lets bury it together or burn it or
set the things that break you out to sea on a little boat
You are loveable
You are worth it
You are my friend

I Missed You On The Train

I missed you on the train years ago
I was supposed to love you but we never met
So our destinies never crossed

You saw my eyes and you knew I was someone you missed
It's hard on you isn't it? You were supposed to feel the way we feel
Now you must run from it
Because we will spill the wine
And make a horrible mess
All because I missed meeting you
And now we have and we cannot put it back
Now you know your heart is out of the cage and will fly
In danger we now live
Because I missed you on that train years ago

Shadow

Friday, February 2, 2018

A shadow of a person you will never meet
A shadow of someone who you will never know
A glimpse of who the might have been to you and never will
All the shadows that break the darkness and the light
He is my shadow
I turn on the light to make him scatter
But then sometimes the hair on my arms stand up
Like goosebumps and I recoil from fear
I never say the right thing
But he is my shadow
He is dark and frightening
Angry without reason
Lonely but happy but sad simultaneously
Hes nice but not
Caring but careless
Hes a shadow
Of all the things that never can be
He's my shadow

The House of Fire and Whispers

In the the Casbah
The walls shook
As Ali La Pointe made up his mind
Then the walls came down
And a victory was proclaimed
and the Casbah became the House of Fire and Whispers
Say my name, call the Fire
I will not hand you my nose
Ali La Point said Here is my destiny
I am but a simple man .perhaps not perfect
But I will rest in the House of Fire and Whispers for you
So the French made the walls come down
Hassiba .. Hassiba.. you held the walls

As it all came down that day
And the victors were not who made it happen
They became ghosts and then the fire started
And became the flame that became Algeria..
So here is to the ones of us
Who disappear in fire and smoke
Who lose to bigger foes
And think that all is lost
I dream to live in a House of Fire and Whispers
And be a legend IIke they were
But I live in books and their memory
In paper and not a fortress
Oh Ali and Hassiba.. I wish you could see

Everything that happened was not in vain
There have been fires and storms that almost won
But you rise like the flames
in our memory
And when I think of you.. I live in the House of Fire and Whispers
Oh Algiers majestic you enchant me
You make me weep that I could be

A simple student or a thief
And save a nation like they did
Oh all of us could dream to be
Prisoners in the House of Fire and Whispers

Under The Moon

under the moon
you held my hand
you touched my face
you were my man
we drove all night
to talk and feel
each others heart
in the moon light
I miss you so
we met too late
in both our lives
it was our fate
under the moon
you held my hand
you touched my face
you were my man
it was never our time
i loved you so
we had to say goodbye
Im letting you go
so just know my heart is with you
though i am far
i remember the night
we kissed in the car
under the moon
you held my hand
you touched my face
you were my man

Return Not To Me

If advice comes with condemnation
Then return not to me
If the only time you care about me
Is if you have an audience
Then return not to me
If you cannot see beauty without naming the ugly
Return not to me, return not to me
If you cannot remember how I struggled
Yet throw more heartbreak on me
Return not to me return not to me
If my breaths were labored and yet you faltered
Return not to me
Better shadows and cold
Than loss I cannot measure
When you added fuel to the fire of what hurt me already
Return not to me
Return not to me

Chariot

Like phoenix from the ashes
You shall have your chariot
Count the years and the days and things will stop to hurt
King oh king you shall have your chariot
Bide your time and count the days , the hours and minutes
And your heart will stop to break
I could fix 1000 things for you and hear all the pain
And organize your thoughts
But so far away can never help
So you shall rise alone
Like phoenix from the ashes you shall have your chariot
My king my king
The pharohs of the east and winds of the water shall find you
As they take you home to heal
But you shall find your chariot
Blue and green
You are precious
My precious friend
You shall find
Your chariot

Swim In That Ocean

Do you want to swim in that ocean
that ocean that can swallow you whole
and sneak up on you as you are swimming
like a scuba diver, you grab your mask disoriented
shaking and cannot stabilize yourself

Do you want to love that uncontrollably?
That loss looks better than lack of possession
Do you want to swim in that ocean
That ocean where if you kiss you might not stop
Or when you breath, they get shallow and pained

Do you want to love that intensely
that love becomes like blood that sticks inside an iv
Brutal and thick, painful and bruising

Do you want to love like driving with the car with the top down
Against the highways wind
The sand blowing inside
And fear over takes you

Do you want to swim in that ocean beloved
Do you want to live to risk it all
To not miss a moment of what love could or should have been

Do you want to swim in that ocean beloved

Do you want to swim in that ocean

If Love Were A Lie

If love were a lie
I might ask you to lie to me
over and over again
If love was just fleeting
And perhaps was not ours to have
I will not dismiss it or make it a small thing
That is not my role or place to say

That it is not real or does not exist
Should I envy it? Or covet it?
If love were a lie?
We need stories
 we need hope
If love were a lie? Should we lie to each other?
Keep hope alive, so that others risk and drown
The best kept secret or perhaps nonsense
However tragic or fatal or impossible
If love were a lie, I might not warn people
Or breathe in the fire of disappointment
If love were a lie

Moroccan Girl

for Bouchra and Nadia

Friday, February 2, 2018

Thank you for saving a space at your table
When Pinhas begins to sing
We will forget all the facts we wrote down a hundred times
Because the ice tastes too cold
When the night has too many stars
Thank you habiba for saving a seat
And we trance dance like gnawa set the speakers on fire
I came to you because of loss and stayed because we both lost
And our friendship grew because we both had nothing else to lose
Best friends and riders on a trail of loss and goodbyes
I will share the blue skies with you
And all the in between times
I love you forever and ever
Moroccan girls

Casa Port

Trains to no where ... here there and everywhere
Casaport said Kathleen.. catch your train
You arent particularly welcome but we are used to you
Lala Amerikaniya.. you talk to much but we know you . come here

Sit here .. stand here go here.. stop here

At Casaport, you fit right in
You are no ones wife, or love , you just are family
You gave birth to one of ours and we will love you meskina

Hop a train or a bus, come to Casablanca darling
Its yours , the bakeries, snack amine, the sea and the trams
The nights and the days and the mornings and evenings
Come lost confused person, Morocco awaits you
On buses to Marrakesh and trains going everywhere

Casaport, ya blatia

Casaport
with hints and secrets and a taxi anywhere else
To Casablanca we go, there s not much evening left
To Casaport, look Im not holding on.. Im riding sitting or standing
To Casaport with your bag.. To Casaport

There Will Come A Day

Tuesday, September 13, 2016

There will come a day

when you will realize what you did

And I don t want to see your crocodile tears

We went on without you
I raised your daughter all alone.. and built the walls around her to be
the ones you broke
I made holidays and eids, brushed hair and laid out outfits, and
calmed fevers
While you ran away from responsibility

there will come a day, when she will be everything you ever wanted
And I always told her you were busy.. or working or gone and that
you didn't reject her

I cleaned up your messes, put the tears away and built a woman

But there will come a day when she will be all you want, her breath
close to yours
Her laughs aligned with yours.

There will come a day.. and its not very far away, when you will need
her and understand
that being selfish got you no where. I never told her not to trust you.
Your absence taught her that

No one kept you from her but your childishness

There will come a day

Aïn Fouara

She spoke in code to talk to friends who might understand
what its like to be as cold as stone
I have turned into the statue at Ain Fouara
Im just like a rock yet water flows out of me
whispering to anyone who comes near.. here is a drink
please take care dear friend.. drink from the well that tells you you
have a place
once again
Im a statue, my skin cold and smooth
My heart beats so faintly you can barely feel the heat
Under my skin
My hearts broken in every possible way but I love people
So I remain a statue in Ain Fouara
Im cold and rounded , stoic and giving
But broken and lost at the same exact time
I long for a place I can never be
I am frightened of a life that is getting harder to bear
Yet I want to love and help and be there for people
Setif I miss you and your streets and your sky
I want to sit in your garden close by Ain Fouara and sit by myself
And remember why I tried to run there to begin with
If only I wasnt a statue trapped in Ain Fouara and I could be free
again to plant flowers and move like the water from the fountain
Im just a ghost in the garden
Or trapped in still motion
At Ain Fouara

Sing to Me of Perfect People

Sing to me of perfect people
Untarnished by life with nothing to be ashamed of
I will show you a person who will not show up in the dead of night
When the buildings are burning and the wolves are circling
Its the thieves and the fallen who stand up to the monsters

The Ali La Pointes...barricading themselves in a nation in the Casbah

The students.... the pirates.. the scared and forgotten

Who have nothing left to lose who save and inspire
The Che Guevaras.. the Maya Angelous

Were not born in perfection
The were forged by pain and loss and disappointments
Oh to be lucky enough to fail in life
To be downtrodden and scared .. to lose over and over again

For they shall be crowned heroes, the imperfect people
The broken and lost.. the mistake ridden souls
Sing to me of perfect people, who never show up
As the buildings are burning
It will be a bad girl who will open her door or answer her phone
When you have no one else to turn
Or someone struggling with alcoholism who has over come the mon-
ster

Who will be the first to say do not worry do not fear
While the good girls and boys scatter like flies, fearful of risk and
fearful of bravery

Fearful of everything including life itself

Sing to me of perfection and I'll show you hypocrisy
I d rather call down the streets to the lost and the scared
And have a friend who will stand by me
Sing to me.. sing to me

Chemaa

You are the candle
And you dance across the walls as a shadow
and then the shadows grow
you are the candle
and hot as you burn.. you will one day cool
and I will hold my hands in front of my face in grief
when your love ends

when the night turns into dawn

You are the candle
whisper your smoke into the evening mist
as I open the window
and jasmine fills the room

You are the candle
And I disappear in your glow
as you break me
You are the candle

Who Was She?

Was she Spanish
Was she anglo
Were her dreams in your eyes as you told her you loved her?

Did your life on the other side flash before you as you looked at her
An affadavit of support?

I saw the announcement... that he fulfilled all his dreams
But I wondered how he crossed the great divide
Did he pass those 3 years quickly? Or were they slow and difficult
Who was she?
Was she old, was she stupid, was she wise , was she broken?
Those dreams you crushed? Were they worthy?
Was it worth it? Did she make it out ok?
Who was she?
Was she broken? Was she nice? Did she start to drink as she realized
it was all a lie?
Who was she?
Did she cry as you began to morph into who you really were?
When the age is just a number all the sudden was the only number
you knew?
When what was useful became worth nothing as the papers began to
move quickly through the system?
Who was she khouya? Who was she?

That Silence Darling Oh That Silence

The things we do inside the silence
We dance to songs that no one can hear
The nights we spend in quiet and we only whisper
Back and forth, to silence we return, all alone in breaths, one after
another

Pausing between them, grasping for air
That silence darling oh that silence

That posseses moments between the words
I will wait for it, over and over
For it to return and broken windows to give way
That silence darling oh that silence
I used to long for words to fill the empty corners of the room

Now with open hands I grab ahold of the nothingness
Late late nights with nothing but silence to spend time with
That silence darling oh that silence

The Sisters of Fatima

I could not find the words or walk past the sadness in my life to
Light a candle to you
I won't be afraid.. you'll be there for me .. when I say goodbye to this
world.. surrounding me on this journey...

But you came and found me
Oh sisters of Fatima
I hung your pictures on her wall... some of drummers
One of weavers

And put three dolls on a shelf.. One was a bride ... the other was ber-
ber
And the magic began to move through my house
The sisters of Fatima were everywhere....

Zahra s eyes glistened as she looked at me
Momma... God gave me to you and your job is to protect and love
The sisters of Fatima ...
So I wept on my sofa.. lost in despair

Where will I find my footing? Where will I find solace?
Open the doors... Tell them that the house of Zahra is open to all
And you will be the fountain and not weep.. but flow...
Not able to find words that flowed together
I would say.. Sisters of Fatima.. sisters of Fatima..
My heart is so sick... look for me.. Ill look for you
With a heart wrapped in fabric and devotion
I stood up... they will not fail me
Her cousins... her family will become mine
Do they want me ? Do they love me? I will love them

I will love them from near and far. I will love them from the North to
the South
I will give them passage, shelter and relief.. out of love for her....
Out of love for her.. I'll never leave them
So that one day as I say good bye this world

I will be surrounded by the sisters of Fatima...
The daughters of Moulay Ismail..
The watchers from the windows..
The sisters of Fatima ....

Moroccan women.. sisters of my beloved Zahra
The sisters of Fatima...

Vapor

like two snakes it rose
like a mist on the ocean
it looked like life but never was
it was mist
only water
never more than water
Vapor
I put my hands into it
And held my fingers around it
but it was only mist
It was fragile and ethereal
and never mine to have
like snakes rising from the ground
the sky the sky it moved
and memories surrounded it
and it was invisible and cautious.. rising faster and faster

like vapor on the ocean
like the night that no longer existed
I am sorry I cried
but the vapor escaped my hands
and like a misspelled binder on a book that caused the book to go un
found
on a bookshelf
the vapor was just that
vapor.. mist and air

never materializing
into anything solid
vapor mist and smoke
it ended

Oh to Be Trapped by Dreams

Oh to be trapped by dreams
Things that never came
As some of us are sold a bill of goods

We won't be wives
We won't be husbands
Some of us are destined to ride trains
To no where
Just serve as stops on a road as others progress on
Some of us have to be ok with never having a happy ending
We mourn what never happened.. or what never will be
Some of us are destined to walk alone
To lose to weep

And there is no solution
But to be brave and hold our heads high
As we lose and lose and lose lose
Some of us are trapped by dreams
Of what can never be

We are noble in these losses.. through these tears
With damaged lives and broken hearts
Some of us are
Trapped by dreams
Holding out hope for answers that will never come
We mourn what can never happen
Even
if we were deserving
Some of us can never win
Oh to be ok in the face of loss
Oh to be ok in the face of things that never appeared
Oh to be never loved
Oh to carry your fate as a woman or a man

Those of us who burn for things that can never be
those of us who disappear in the flames of what might have been
loss becomes a pyre
upon which we lay
oh to be
oh to be
Oh to be never wanted

Biography

Kathleen is the mother of three and lives in Orlando Florida. She has spent the last few years helping Algerian and Moroccan immigrants. She was a victim of severe spousal abuse and in 2008 lost her son Rayan Mehdi and has used music and poetry to survive the loss of her son.